THROWING THE BONES

CINDY RHODES

DEDICATION

This book is dedicated with gratitude
to the Spirit that
dwells within us all.
May we keep silent in order to
hear and follow the
voice of Wisdom at all times.

CONTENTS

ACKNOWLEDGMENTS

Thank you so much,
my dear teachers, my dear clients, my dear husband, my
dear vast spiritual family, my close inner circle, and the
Spirit that guides us all, if only we listen.

1 DIVINATION

For centuries, man has desired to communicate with that beautiful invisible Force that knows all. The reason? Man wants to be relieved of the pain of unknowing and settle his gnawing questions. "Where have I been? Where am I going? Is my life course the right one? Will I ever meet a truly compatible life partner? What's wrong with me?" All these questions have.been asked by us at some point in our lives.

We believe that the answers to our questions lie with the Divine. The word "divination," in fact, emerges from a form of the word "divine," meaning "relating to God." The Divine Word, as mentioned in the Bible in the first verse of the Greek Book of John, is described within these words: "In the beginning was the Word, and the Word was with God."

Without spending time with the debate of whether the Word "was" God, "with" God, or "a god," we may simply understand that the main point of the communication here is that knowledge has been made available to us via a spiritual channel. It is by communing with the Divine Spirit that we may understand Its messages and guidance for us, and the Word is just that – the generously provided messages and guidance that is available to us all.

In contemporary cultures of the more "advanced" nations, divination is regarded sometimes as archaic and silly. Many use the word "evil" to label the act of beseeching the Spirit for answers. However, the same people who would condemn or disregard the act of divination will also chant memorized prayers to invisible deities and then look for the materialization of their prayers to appear in their lives.

In fact, when church-goers ask how to obtain answers from God, the instruction that they receive from many established religions is to "pray, listen, and look." Pastors, rabbis, reverends, priests, and their colleagues will instruct a "seeker" to offer up questions to God and then wait patiently for the answer, which comes in the form of a voice or a sign. The only difference between seeking answers through prayer and in seeking answers with divination is the use of tools.

One method of divination recorded in the Hebrew Scriptures of the Bible is the use of the Urim and Thummim. The Urim and Thummim have been described in different ways, some conflicting, but the point of using the Urim and Thummim was to divinely determine God's will, guilt or innocence, ancestry, and yes/no answers by looking at the results that they offered. The Urim and the Thummim were considered sacred tools, and the High Priest frequently stored these two tools inside a highly elaborate breast plate made of gold embedded with precious stones. These two tools, depicting opposites such as light and dark, positive and negative, perfection and imperfection, were no doubt not the very first divinatory tools, but they certainly were the most published and examined in Biblical studies.

When researching methods of divination, one will discover that the list is a long one. One interesting list of divination practices and the signs read in these practices is as follows:

Aeromancy: atmospheric conditions
Alectormancy: birds
Alphitomancy: effects of eating prepared bread
Arithmancy: numbers
Astrology: celestial bodies
Bibliomancy: randomly chosen book passages
Carromancy: melting wax
Cartomancy: cards
Cheiromancy: hands, fingers, and nails
Cyclomancy: spinning bottles or tops
Dendromancy: oak or mistletoe
Dowsing: bending rod that locates water
Fractomancy: fractals
Gematria: numerical values of letters and words
Geomancy: cartographical lines
Gyromancy: twirling and falling upon an answer
Hieromancy: burnt offerings
Ichthyomancy: fish entrails
Lithomancy: crystals and stones

Metoposcopy: forehead wrinkles
Moleosophy: moles on one's body
Necromancy: communication with the dead
Oculomancy: formations in the eye
Oenomancy: wine
Oneiromancy: dreams
Oomancy: eggs
Osteomancy: bones
Podomancy: feet
Pyromancy: fire
Radiesthesia: pendulum
Scrying: perceived visions in water, a mirror, etc.
Selenomancy: moon phases and appearance
Sideromancy: shapes formed by heated straws
Spasmatomancy: convulsions
Stareomancy: elements of earth, air, fire, water
Sternomancy: marks on the solar plexus
Sycomancy: drying leaves
Tasseography: tea leaves, coffee grounds, etc.
Tiromancy: the holes in cheese
Trochomancy: wheel ruts and tracks
Umbilicomancy: the umbilical cord
Zoomancy: animals

Within virtually every single spiritual path, some method of divination exists. The "tools" used in these practices range from elevated imagery as with simple cloud formations (as in nephelomancy) to more earthly images as with the physical properties of the bottoms of our feet (as in pedomancy). The most popular forms of divination are ages old and are easily understood because of their use of message-laden "keys," the physical divining elements that represent specific spiritual qualities or messages.

The practice of casting runes, in which one prayerfully throws or selects overturned runes – stone or wooden chips upon which the Norse, Germanic, or other alphabet is inscribed – entails "reading" or interpreting the messages and meanings of the alphabets selected. This method of divination is quite popular with those who follow a Nordic path. The answers sought usually focus around material gain and relationship status, and the physical runes lend themselves quite well to this, as their wooden or stone composition inherently possess a "grounding" quality for both the reader and the querent (the client or person seeking the answers). For the well-grounded and practical reader and querent, the runes are a perfect divination method.

The use of the Tarot cards, reportedly developed from playing cards in Italy around the fifteenth century, provides the reader with answers through cards that represent spiritual qualities that are illustrated with symbolic pictures. Each of the cards represents a specific spiritual quality, and the reader and querent will do well to remember this. Some readers will attempt to assign physical qualities to the cards, but it is only the well-seasoned reader who can do this successfully. The key to success with Tarot is twofold: first, understanding the spiritual messages represented by the pictures and, secondly, understanding the hints at physical answers as delivered spiritually, psychically, to the reader. Also, as with any type of divination, the reader's own spiritual state is of prime importance.

The pendulum is a divination tool of choice when one desires a "yes/no" answer. The pendulum is usually made of materials that are spiritually important to the reader, and the reader will spend time dedicated to "attuning" himself to the pendulum, a practice in which the reader aligns the pendulum's swing with his own mental, psychological, and spiritual vibrations or wavelengths. Any person who desires to learn how to obtain quick, reliable "yes/no" answers can easily obtain a special pendulum and learn how to attune himself to it and "read" its answers. This makes the pendulum one of the most popular instruments of divination today.

For answers that hold symbolic imagery relating to the past, present, or future, the divining practice of tasseography is well-suited. This practice of reading tea leaves involves the brewing of tea while conversing with a querent. The reader uses the conversation to "draw out" the client's questions and apprehensions, allowing spiritual influence to begin its work. The spiritual images that appear to the reader in the form of tea leaves in the bottom of the empty tea cup reveal the answers to the querent's questions. It is the highly visually-oriented reader who has the best success with tasseography, and it is the querent with a deep appreciation for symbolic imagery who will also appreciate the answers that are derived.

These most popular forms of divination involve asking questions with material answers, spiritual answers, yes/no answers, or visual answers, but one form of divination that manages to incorporate all of these is the act of throwing the bones. This is not to say that none of the others can combine forms of answers; answers revealed and the methods in which the messages are revealed are completely up to the reader's own level of spirituality and expertise. The problem for the novice, though, is knowing just where to find a good teacher who is also a well-practiced diviner of spiritual knowledge, and not one who just scratches the mundane surface.

Contemporary interest in the divining tools of old has formed in the hearts of new followers of both mainstream spiritual paths and offbeat pagan paths as well. Interested ones desire more information about every detail about throwing the bones, but nothing existed until recent publications and sharing of information on social media channels. It is this author's desire to share in-depth knowledge, insight, and techniques in order to help a potential future thrower-of-bones to develop a style that is both accurate and ethical.

As with every form of divination, the reader's experience tends to add depth to the many spiritual layers to the answers that can be revealed through one's chosen form of divination. Since the quality of the results lie with the experience of the reader and the expectation of the querent, we need to remember that to begin answering the call to throw the bones, it is necessary to inspect all involved: the reader ("sangoma"), the querent, the "ground," the "bones, and everything else involved. Every blessing upon each of you and upon your tools!

2 THE SANGOMA

The very first requirement for throwing the bones is a wise person to actually serve as an effective reader. One who is just beginning will want to practice with his own immediate questions first, perhaps many times, before feeling proficient enough to practice with a trusted friend. As he gains experience with throwing the bones, it becomes more and more clear that the reader's level of spirituality will dictate the "depth" of the reading; this practice is not for the mundane or profane. As with any type of divination, the reader must be one who is spiritually "connected" enough to discern answers as they appear in shapes and patterns, mature enough to understand the import and potential effects of the messages upon the querent, and loving enough to deliver difficult answers in tactful ways.

Who was the first person to "throw the bones?" Archeology suggests that this practice could have been initiated by African shamanic healers. By casting actual bones, shells, and other natural objects, the advanced spiritual healer, or "sangoma," could diagnose illness and discover an effective method of treatment, usually requiring a spiritual act, gift, or sacrifice from the querent or his family. His status as sangoma was greatly respected.

The sangoma devoted his entire life to the honoring of the Spirit. In fact, everyone in his community expected him to do this. They supported his Spirit-directed life and ensured the continued nurturing of their spiritual welfare by honoring and supporting his life and lineage. The skulls of past sangomas, the ancestors of the current sangoma, were treated with reverence, anointed, painted, and used in the bone rituals of divination. Serving as a "High Priest" to his community, the sangoma cherished his connection to the Spirit that led his people.

So, too, today's potential bone readers must be authentically devoted to honoring Spirit and living up to the calling that they have accepted. If one is not "connected" to Spirit, how will one communicate with It? To maintain and nurture one's connection to Spirit, the reader must be well-read, open, and willing, and his spiritual connection must be pure. The "connected" reader will begin and end his day with a prayerful attitude and walk throughout his day without losing that spiritual connection, understanding that every moment is an opportunity for spiritual growth on his part. Blatant immaturity and less-than-lofty motives will always sully one's spiritual connection. The devoted sangoma will be diligent in his daily spiritual routine and work toward two objectives: to do the best that he can for every single person who comes to him and to be the best living example that he can in order to represent the Spirit spotlessly.

The maturity and experience of the ancient sangoma would determine the depth and import of the messages received. If one had not experienced the "climate" of war, then how could he fully understand any spiritual messages about war? If one had not experienced the raising of children, how could he fully understand spiritual messages about children? If one had not experienced the agony of self-realization, the admission of imperfection, and the ecstasy of becoming a mature person, how could he fully understand the spiritual messages for those who were growing past the bloom of youth? If one had not experienced the pangs of emotion, how could he fully understand the spiritual messages pertaining to joy, grief, and desire?

So, too, today's potential reader must pay attention to developing maturity on all levels: spiritually, emotionally, intellectually, and physically. To do this, the reader must remain humble enough to receive spiritual correction, balanced enough to maintain his mundane needs, and loving enough to administer kindly to others. Just as awakening with a prayerful attitude can keep one connected to Spirit, it can also help one to develop maturity as he receives and meditates upon spiritual messages that come to him each day.

The reader must, too, be a loving individual. Love is the most powerful force in the universe; it is one of creativity, constructiveness, and nurture. If one does not hold a loving, altruistic, nurturing attitude toward life, his neighbor, or himself, then his readings will be completely useless, chaotic, and perhaps even harmful. One who was truly connected in olden days, the Apostle Paul, wrote in his first letter to the Corinthians (chapter thirteen) that anyone who delivers a sign or prophecy without the spirit of love will be delivering a useless message. He writes: "If I speak in tongues of men or angels, but do not have love, I am only a resounding gong or a clanging cymbal. If I have the gift of prophecy and can fathom all mysteries and all knowledge, and if I have a faith that can move mountains, but do not have love, I am nothing."

The entire reason for a reader's spending his time and energy in delivering messages to a querent is what? Is it to make money? No. It is to create fame for oneself? No. The purpose of reading the bones is to deliver spiritually-borne messages and guidance to querents so that they can make healthful decisions, become mature in their thinking, maintain balance in their lives, and strengthen their spiritual Selves. Any direction, message, or guidance that veers from this purpose is potentially useless.

A truly loving reader will nurture the spirit of love and always keep the querent's best interest in mind. He will have the ability to understand the weight of his words and their effect upon the querent. He will never use his words to cause harm or create chaos.

As communal spirit ruled most ancient African tribal cultures, possessiveness and materialism were no doubt present, but possibly not as pervasive as today. With mostly questions about health, fertility, productiveness and spirituality being offered up, mundane questions were the exception rather than the rule. The sheer quest for survival created issues much more important than some of today's frequently asked questions. Education and guidance as to how to thrive and survive as a human being in a community is the information most ancients sought and these issues are certainly worth looking into today. The larger-than-life issues of alchemical quests (personal perfection) and sheer survival (a concern inherent to the species) take precedence over the majority of questions that are asked today. To ask a frivolous question can actually be a disrespectful act toward the Spirit.

The ancient sangoma might have experienced great disregard for those who would pester Higher Powers with mundane questions. However, today's society has unfortunately become so immersed in the material and mundane that such questions are expressed to contemporary readers with wild abandon. "When is he going to text me back? Is he thinking about me? Am I going to meet my soul mate?" These types of questions can belabor a reader who is ready to dispense valuable spiritual answers. The kind and wise reader, however, in his desire to ease the querent's spiritual dis-ease, will find a way to reveal the true spiritual answer to the querent's questions, answering the question but giving more than the querent asked for; he will find a way to reveal WHY the querent seeks such an answer and what can be done in order to heal one's spiritual sickness.

The most important thing to remember when throwing the bones is that the act itself is a sublimely respectful and spiritual practice, and the reader needs to take great care not to "grieve the Spirit," or ask disrespectful questions. Maturity, wisdom, and experience will be the reader's best friends in situations in which taxing questions are asked. Therefore, it is very important for the reader to be someone who engages in an ongoing process of introspection and continual quest to follow in the path that Spirit leads him. By engaging in this never-ending practice, the reader will have discovered within himself the answers that his querents seek!

Too, the state of the reader's mind, heart, body, and spirit must be in line with Spirit in order to commune with It. A good reader will be continually engaged in avenues of higher learning. The one who reads and studies subjects of spiritual healing, spiritual communication, and spiritual paths will be the one who makes the best reader with throwing the bones. One who throws the bones but neglects opportunities to obtain further spiritual instruction is only cheating himself and his querents. The practice of throwing the bones can uncover such a wide variety of subjects that unless one is adequately educated, one cannot give an educated answer, and, as it is the querent's best interest that we seek, the reader would do himself and the querent a disservice should he neglect his spiritual studies.

Daily meditation is the perfect companion to daily study and practice. Creating and maintaining a ritual of meditation will help the reader to fully develop his spiritual personality and maintain what is needed to fulfill his calling. Answering the "call" to fulfill one's spiritually-divined ordination is the highest, most rewarding objective that one can pursue in one's life. The devoted, serious reader will acknowledge this and embrace it.

No one can ultimately say who the first people were to throw the bones. What we can ultimately say is that the very human desire to know the seemingly unknown will inspire him to seek those answers from what is immediately around him. His desire, coupled with his reliance on assistance of that Unseen Force, will bring forth the appropriate method of divining the answers that lie within one's Higher Self and from his particular vision of the Divine.

Whatever your level of spirituality, if you desire to seriously take up the calling of throwing the bones, you must also take up the vast responsibility of furthering your spiritual development. Hearing the call is a sign in itself, a sign that you are progressing in a positive spiritual way. Continue studying. Continue your spiritual practices. Grow. Learn. Mature. This is how you will be transformed from a simple "reader" to a full-fledged sangoma, a true healer, and eventually, a true sangoma.

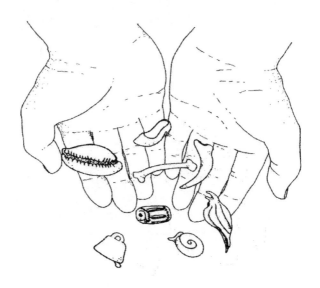

3 THE GROUND

Once a blossoming reader has decided to answer the call and readied himself, he must decide upon a "ground" upon which to throw the bones. This must truly be the most sacred ground in his life, as it is a place that he will reverently reserve solely for his divination. Much as a game board defines space for a game, the "bone ground" will define the area where the reader will always throw the bones.

The ground for throwing bones can be a special piece of fabric, an open box, or a circular serving tray. It can even be a place in the sand if the area is drawn with the sangoma's finger or a wand set aside solely for this purpose. The open box and serving trays are wonderful for containing the bones and preventing them from falling off the table in the case of the new reader's over-zealousness, but if one expects to throw the bones multiple times, the ground needs to be large enough to accommodate one's hands scooping down to collect the bones for another throw.

For the past several years, my favorite throwing ground consists of a large shallow serving tray lined with a special divining pad that I sewed especially for this purpose. The lip of the tray prevents losing any errant bones, and the soft quilted ground, complete with certain markings, serves as a perfect, soft platform for divination. The soft surface preserves the integrity of my bone pieces, and the markings provide a standard of marking time and space, giving me a method of developing a time line and predicting a series of events.

To create a very personalized throwing ground, select one or two natural fabrics with complementary designs and patterns. One may certainly use manmade fabrics, but natural fabrics decorated with natural dyes make the best ground, as "natural" is always better. The aim of choosing the fabric is to feel spiritually bonded with your choices.

For example, people who identify with water signs might appreciate choosing fabrics with aquatic life designs. Fire signs might enjoy blazing colors. Earth signs might prefer landscape or plant designs, and Air signs might choose cloudscapes and birds. A reader who is familiar with his astrological chart might choose a fabric for his Sun sign and a fabric for his Moon sign.

Any pattern that appeals to the reader will be perfect, but one that is quite profound is the spiral, symbolic of swirling energy being drawn down to the earth for use in the reading. In the Northern Hemisphere, the counterclockwise spiral is directional pattern in which energy is drawn to the earth; the word "widdershins" applies to this counterclockwise motion and indicates a "pulling" of energy downward.

To create the spiral upon the fabric ground, we begin by cutting a circular piece of fabric. A circle that is about 18 inches in diameter is a perfect size to accommodate the bones with some comfortable space left over. Starting on the outside edge of the circle, draw the spiral in a counterclockwise fashion until the pencil point ends in the center.

If the reader desires to have his ground made of just one fabric, then the spiral may be embroidered with contrasting colors so that it is easily seen during the reading (See Figure 1). If the reader desires to have two fabrics for his ground, then he may create the spiral by placing a piece of fabric upon the drawn line and appliqueing it upon the base fabric (See Figure 2). The desired effect is one of a spiral that ends in the center of the circular ground.

Embroidering or appliqueing the design is a process that will be well worth the time and effort of doing it by hand. Hand sewing helps to connect and bind the reader to his ground as he diligently works to create the most spiritually meaningful ground that he can. Having soft, meditative instrumental music playing in the room as one sews, one can achieve a grand meditative state and produce a throwing ground that can be used forever with significant and meaningful results.

Fig. 1.   Fig. 2.

Other markings may be embroidered onto the ground, if one desires to have a distinct "time line" upon it. The markings are like those of a bull's eye, and each segment will indicate a period of time – an hour, a day, week, month, year, or more, depending upon the general "feel" of the answer that is given to any time-sensitive question.

If one does desire a "time line," then one may use concentric circles within the body of the ground. The thread used for embroidery, if of a second color in contrast to the one used for the original sewing, will stand out nicely during the reading. Figures 3 and 4 show this result.

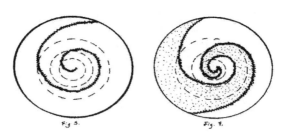

Fig 3.   Fig. 4.

For cardinal directions, one may certainly include a compass rose or even embroidered lines to divide the circular ground into four quadrants. This type of delineation is helpful for questions pertaining to where one should move, where a lost object lies in wait, and where one will meet someone new. These lines, however, are not mandatory, and when I am asked to throw the bones on these topics, I keep the imaginary compass rose in mind when delivering my answers. One decorative way to denote the cardinal directions, however, is to embroider the initials of the directions, N, E, S, and W, in their prospective locations upon the edge of the ground. This will keep the central area "less busy" and provide decorative touches on the outer edge of the ground. The placement of the compass points also ensures that one is conscientiously placing it properly upon the table, ensuring accurate directional answers. See Figure 5 for an illustration of the embroidered compass points on a ground with contrasting fabrics.

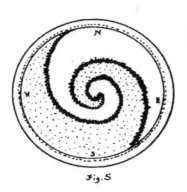

Fig. 5

Once the inner embroidery is completed, the outside edge must be secured in some way, either with an elementary blanket stitch to prevent fraying or with a piece of binding tape or grosgrain fabric. The blanket stitch is particularly useful as it allows the sangoma to employ handwork to the ground. Grosgrain fabric or binding tape, though, are certainly just as easily functional as they involved securely sewing the binding on top of the ground edges that are folded over to create a smooth, protected edge. The objective of finishing the edge is to protect the ground from fraying, thus preserving it for a very long time. Such a cherished spiritual tool deserves to have a fine finish.

The most important thing to remember when creating your throwing ground is that this ground is truly sacred. It deserves the finest materials, and it deserves your best work. Fabrics of fine quality and of appropriate color and design will provide a pleasing, familiar space as you read the bones, and threads in symbolic colors, as well, will add to the depth of your readings. As every spiritually advanced practitioner knows, we reap what we sow, and, in the case of creating a throwing ground, we reap what we "sew."

4 THE BONES

Of all the "ingredients" needed to throw the bones, the most esoterically-chosen and symbolically-laden are the "bones" themselves. These objects are the esoteric equivalent to runes and Tarot cards. To the untrained eye they might look like mere shells, beans, bones, seeds, or other miniature trinkets, but each one holds an esoteric meaning of great importance.

The thoughtful reader will take great care in choosing just the right objects for his own personal set of "bones." Small objects which hold no importance to others might represent a major event or spiritual idea to the reader. Choosing one's "bones" requires a spiritual mindset and a high capacity for visualization as he assigns a spiritual quality to each object."

As the reader prepares to collect the bones for his personal set, he should make a list of many different esoteric ideas and life events that will be considered in every reading. If the reader is familiar with Tarot cards and runes, he may decide to choose bone elements that correspond to some of those familiar esoteric topics. However, he will also want to include some additional objects to represent other common topics.

When a reader begins, it would be best to keep things simple and choose only five or six bones for practice. However, once he becomes well practiced with these few objects, he will quickly want to add more and more "bones" to his pile as he gains experience. When I began throwing the bones, I only kept about ten objects in my bone set, and I was able to read issues about travel, finances, best friends, jobs, homes, death, marriage partners, education, projects, and gifts. Through the years, however, my growing practice demanded more elaborate and idiosyncratic symbols. I now sometimes use more than twenty objects in my readings, and the depth of my readings is much greater!

When deciding on which topics and which objects to use, try to "feel" what each object "says" to you. Then consider what the opposite of that esoteric symbol might be. A small toy car, for instance, might mean to you that someone will be getting a new car soon, and if it were to land upside down in a reading, it might be an indicator of car problems. The porcelain arm of a doll might represent strength if it lands in one direction, and muscle weakness if it lands in another. A sterling silver fish pendant might seem to represent life if it lands right side up, but it might seem to signify death, or travel to the afterlife, if it were to land upside down, with its hollow back showing.

A reader's bones are vastly personal to him. No one else will perceive the very same symbolic meaning in an object, as between strangers vast nuances in spiritual perceptions exist. Tarot cards and runes both represent "set" standards and symbols that anyone can perceive, and anyone can choose cards or throw runes and decipher their messages according to set layouts, and their owners become "bonded" to their Tarot and rune sets. However, with throwing the bones, the reader also becomes "bonded" with his set of bones, but each bone is as unique to him as his fingerprint. No reader's bones will be the same as another's! This is just one of the many reasons for the amount of intrigue and interest associated with throwing the bones.

When making one's list of esoteric symbols, it is good to think about the major issues of life. To start, one might include symbols for the following topics:

> Romance
> Travel
> Health
> Money
> Job
> Children
> Friends
> Death
> Education
> Marriage

Then, as the reader becomes more experienced, he might decide to add such topics as these:

> Legal issues
> Real estate

Music or talent
Long distance travel
Moving
Communication (phone call, text, etc.)
Automotive issues
Spirit Guides
Men
Women
Family dynamics
Adoption
International currency
Ex-lovers
Religion
Issues of the elderly
Engagement
Siblings
Deceased relatives
Bonuses
Parties
Bodies of water
Pregnancies
Vacations
Incarceration
Sexual attraction
Mental health issues
Pets

The objects that one chooses to represent each topic can be made of just about anything. Tiny toys, charms, actual bones, stones, shells, game pieces, die, buttons, sticks, coins, and beads can provide a wide variety of objects from which to choose. A tiny doll's white shoe can symbolize a wedding. A gem from an old lover's gift can symbolize the return of a lover. A pink heart-shaped button can symbolize true love when it is right-side-up and a breakup when it is upside down. A few tiny pearls beads can symbolize the appearance of children. A piece of coral that looks like a brain can represent an educational opportunity. Almost anything can be used as a "bone" in a bone reading.

The only real limit that must be placed upon the bones is their weight and dimension. A wise person would not want to include a 2-ounce lead weight, for instance, as it would be much too heavy to accommodate with the other objects and could actually damage the other objects during a throwing, or "casting." Objects that are smaller than the size of a quarter (25 cents USA) are perfect. If you can imagine holding in your hands twenty objects as you throw the bones, you can also see why "smaller is better" when choosing objects.

Another reason for choosing smaller objects is that they will need to be stored in a convenient holder of some type. Ornate boxes, abalone shells, velvet pouches, and any type of special holder will do. I personally love my abalone shell. I place the bones inside the shell, and then I place the whole thing into a sheer mesh bag. The mesh bag, to me, represents the Spirit World, the Esoteric Veil. When I remove the bones from this bag, it is as if they have "crossed the Veil" and are now ready to transmit messages from the Other Side.

Before beginning to throw the bones for the first

time, remember to thoughtfully and prayerfully collect your unique set of bones and meditate upon each one's symbolism. Prepare their protective container or pouch and place the bones inside. Place them in a sacred space with your unique sacred "ground" and dedicate these objects to a Higher Purpose. From this moment forward, they are no longer simple beads, toys, buttons, stones, or bones. They are sacred tools with which you will disseminate spiritual guidance. Too, remember that you now have in your possession a way to nurture and guide genuine seekers of knowledge and guidance. These tools will help you to fulfill the higher calling of assisting querents to become stronger, happier, and wiser.

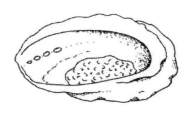

5 THE QUERENT

Imagine, if you will, a small child in desperate need of an answer. He is despondent because his money, by accident, has fallen through a drainage grate. Without this money, he cannot buy the ice cream that he craves. He has a genuine need, and he is an honest "seeker" when he approaches you for assistance. You provide loving answers and assistance when you explain why the coins fell through the grate and what is needed to retrieve the coins from such a distance. The result of your meeting together is sheer joy and relief as the child skips away to successfully retrieve the coins with proper assistance. The child returns with a thank-you and perhaps two cones of ice cream, one of them for you. In this beautiful case, an honest seeker who seeks answers with love and trust is answered by one who answers in love and trust. The honest seeker responds with gratitude and shows it with a symbol of that gratitude in his sharing of his possessions. This is how the perfect reading falls into place.

Now imagine a little child who has intentionally destroyed a toy. Out of the chaotic destructive force of his own temper, he has completely obliterated the object of his affection. There is no way to reproduce the toy or the positive emotional experiences associated with the ownership of that toy, but the child comes to you anyway, whining for assistance, begging you to help find the toy. Your heart strings respond, and you do all that you can to help, only to be met with dissidence, deference, and disdain. Your own trust of others will not allow you to entertain the thought that the child is a very psychologically and spiritually unbalanced person who denies his own responsibility for his own situation and insists on believing his own lie. As you reveal the truth, the child directs his anger toward you, saying that you are mean and know nothing. There is no finding the toy, but the child refuses to let go of his lie. The lying child becomes more disdainful, and the reader becomes disheartened. This is a perfect catastrophe, and it is a shame when some people act like this, asking for answers but not asking for them in love and trust.

In any relationship, be it a romance, seller/consumer, lawyer/client, doctor/patient, or any other symbiotic relationship, honesty and authenticity are paramount. This is true, too, in the sangoma/querent relationship. Any person who comes to you with honesty, with genuine need and with a pure heart will receive the answers that he seeks. Any person who comes with anything less than that will reap what he sows, and his spirit of intention can affect the less-than-grounded sangoma as well.

Never, ever regret refusing unworthy querents. These are people who will be unhappy no matter what is generously given to them, and the soft-hearted sangoma can become broken-hearted when he finds that he is unable to provide what he thinks that the querent needs. Maturity and experience can help the wise sangoma size up the querent and determine actual honest need, or the lack of it.

When new readers begin assisting others, he will find that most querents are honestly seeking helpful answers. These honest seekers, and the joy that results from helping them, provide beautiful moral support to any reader who has been reading all day long and is tired. Every success seems to inject into the sangoma the ability to give "just one more" reading, one after another, as the resultant elation fuels our energy in preparation for the next honest seeker.

Always remember that anyone who does not respect what you are doing does not belong in the reading. The Spirit that fuels the reading will not work if there is no love or honesty between both parties. Do not forget that giving gifts of spiritual energy and insight to those who do not appreciate it is like throwing pearls to swine.

Therefore, do not feel bad about refusing to throw the bones for "entertainment." Do not feel bad about not throwing the bones for those who come to you time and time again with the same question, as their actions show that they are not embracing the answers in the first place; these are people who are like the second child, the one who really only wanted you to give them attention and pull you into their unholy insanity. Do not feel bad about refusing to throw the bones for those who just want you to "prove" yourself and your skills.

Do not feel bad, either, about refusing a client who wants to know if his romantic interest is going to text him in the next five minutes. Sangomas are not mind readers and the bones are not meant to tell what a person is thinking; what we CAN do is to examine and explain the aspirations and inspirations of certain people in certain situations, and only if we are able to "read energy." To use the bones to determine frequency of communication for an obsessed person is like answering a child who asks "why" every five minutes. That question is superficial, pointless, harrowing, and disrespectful to the Spirit.

Ninety nine percent of all querents come to the sangoma with honest need. These are people who honestly need, desire, and deserve spiritual assistance. Their areas of need will lie in the matters of mostly these topics:

1. How to manifest healthy relationships
2. How to generate wealth
3. How to realize career and vocational goals
4. How to weather crises
5. How to let go of toxic situations
6. How to better themselves

When the honest querent approaches the sangoma with these issues, it is important to listen closely and determine the core need. The querent will always reveal their true need either in their actual words or in the tone of their question. The experienced sangoma will know quickly

1. If the querent is truly in need.
2. If a spiritual answer can truly be given.
3. If the sangoma is qualified to help them.

We must remember that throwing the bones is an age-old practice of divination and that we are to behave honorably at all times. We behave honorably when we honor the Spirit, that Great Force that propels us all. Therefore, first, warmly welcome querents who come in honesty, with honest need, and pure hearts. Secondly, be honest with yourself as to your abilities; if you are not experienced enough to help them, then honestly admit it and refer them to another reader. Give both the Spirit and the querent your best.

6 THE READING

Throwing the bones for the first time is exciting! The objects, as they shift for position inside your cupped hands, seem to possess a vital energy all their own. When you throw the bones for the first time, you will no doubt either throw with too much force or with too little. The first few "throws" are all about becoming acquainted with your bones. Do not worry, though; when a devoted reader sets out to adopt this method of divination, it does not take long for him to "become one" with the process.

To begin, collect your items (bones, container, and ground) and place them on a table in front of you as you sit down. Consider the impact and importance of what you are about to do, and meditate upon this for a moment. If your path includes lighting certain candles for Deity, lighting candles would certainly be a wonderful thing to do at this point.

After meditating on what you are about to do, say a prayer or perform your usual ritual to connect with your Higher Power and become centered and grounded. A regular spiritual routine such as this will help the sangoma to reach the necessary certain spiritual mindset each time he sits down to read anew. Make a note of including your meditation and ritual as the very first thing that you do when beginning to throw the bones.

Once you have completed your meditation, place the container of bones off to the side. Perform this, and every action, with respect. Pick up the throwing ground that you made and place it on the table before you, as you would a dinner plate.

Situate the throwing ground in a way so that when you look upon it, the spiral draws your attention toward the center. This is how our eyes should naturally move when we cast a reading. Before even thinking about throwing bones on this ground, become familiar with it.

Notice the different sets of delineations and decide for yourself what they mean. You alone are the one who must determine what a "day" looks like. You alone are the one who must visualize the spiral of a person's life that is represented on the ground.

Few people learn to thrown the bones before learning how to perform other types of divination. Most people begin with either runes or the Tarot. If you have any experience with these, you will be familiar with the level of spiritual visualization that a reader must possess and develop. Use your own skills with visualization to make spiritual and mental connections with the throwing ground, and be determined to remember those connections referring to time and space. Visualize what a straight time line looks like on your ground. Then visualize a spiral one, understanding that more than one event can happen in a single time frame. Realize the need to be flexible as each reading brings forth its unique message.

Do not rush this time of "bonding" and "attuning" yourself with your throwing ground. This ground is your sacred ground, and it sets the stage for every reading. Be thankful for the opportunity to learn how to perform this type of divination, and be thankful for life itself. Realize that by taking up this practice, you are devoting yourself to a higher spiritual course in life, and dedicate yourself to living with higher standards than before. This moment denotes a change in your life! Then, when you have meditated on and realized the importance of this event, you may begin your first practice reading.

Using cupped hands, gather up the bones and allow them to sit in your cupped hands for a while. Feel their weight and mass. Be determined not to try to "force" the way that they are to fall out of your hands. Then, prayerfully and respectfully, "throw the bones" by projecting them a short distance away from your hands. Only a small amount of effort is necessary to successfully cast them.

Mainly, remember that the center of the ground represents the "here and now," and, therefore, aim for the center. The only determined action that we take with throwing the bones is this very action of aiming for the center. Everything else that follows is merely a result of chance and circumstance.

Once you have cast your bones onto the ground, look at what lies in the center. The symbols that rest here define and describe the situation that lies before you. If you see your object representing marriage, then the way that it is situated will symbolize what is to come regarding marriage. If the central piece carries with it the spiritual theme of education, then the way that it sits upon the ground will reveal the "outcome" or concern on the topic of education.

The objects that lie in the area immediately surrounding the center will symbolize situations that will affect the main topic. If "marriage" is in the center, then "marriage is the main topic. The surrounding objects will reveal what sort of atmosphere and influences will revolve around one's marriage. For instance, if the symbol for a long lost lover is next to the "marriage" object, then it quite possibly means that the querent is going to have to deal with the emotional pangs that are left over from a past relationship, one that has been difficult to understand or accept.

The objects that lie on the outskirts of the ground are not of immediate importance, but they could possibly indicate important issues that could arise in the future. It is a good thing to mention the issues that sit even on the outskirts because this gives the querent an opportunity to practice thinking ahead and preparing himself for the unknown.

A practice question for this exercise is this: "What is the most important issue in my life today? What should I pay the most attention to?" Gather up the bones, reflect upon that question, and then throw the bones. The location of the objects on the ground will determine your answer. What is in the center? That is your main concern. Everything else revolves around it in some way, some ways more important than others. Use your spiritual skills to determine the answers: this is the one thing that no one can teach you! You will learn to rely on your own perceptions as delivered by Spirit!

When you have looked at all of the objects that lay on the ground before you and have asked yourself how each one could affect the main topic, then it is time for the next practice throw. For this one, you will want to ask yourself about something in your future. For instance, if you have a genuine spiritual need for a new car, then gather up the bones into your cupped hands. Holding them respectfully, think concentrate on the question "Is a new car in my future?" and then throw the bones. Where the "car" object lands will determine when that new vehicle is to come to you.

It is this very same technique that we can use to determine when houses will sell, when someone will contact us, when we will finally be able to publish a best seller, and when anything that we can think of can happen. The further away from the center, the further into the future it is. The closer to the center, the sooner that it will appear.

If you have selected a "bone" to represent a move from one place to another, a good practice question for this exercise is such: "When am I going to move from this area?" Gather up the bones, reflect upon the question, and then throw the bones. The location of the objects on the ground will determine your answer. Look at where the object for the move lies. Is it near the center? Then it is soon! Is it on the outskirts? Then it is in the distant future. Is it between the center and edges? If so, see if you can "feel" how much time this represents. It could represent any amount of time – days, weeks, months, and even years. The answer will depend upon your own spiritual perception.

You will enjoy designing other questions that pertain directly to your life. If you need help coming up with questions, think about your life now. Do you have questions about your job? Your family life? Your spiritual life? Your spiritual health? When you decide which question to ask, always gather up the bones respectfully in your cupped hands, prayerfully consider the question, and then cast the bones with an aim toward the center.

One excellent way to practice is to practice on yourself with regard to the questions that most querents ask. Ask yourself if you can use spiritual guidance in manifesting healthy relationships, generating wealth, realizing career and vocational goals, weathering crises, letting go of toxic situations, and bettering yourself. With each question, honestly throw the bones for yourself, and see what spiritual answers come to your heart as you look upon the bones on your sacred ground.

As you become more experienced with throwing the bones, you will perceive deeper spiritual messages in the forms of patterns and shapes. Recognizing patterns and shapes is what the human mind is designed to do! Even as children, we look into the clouds and see past the formations of air and suspended water, picking out animals, objects, people, and symbols, and everything that we see symbolizes something and holds an esoteric meaning for us. This is because humans as a species develop esoteric references to every object that comes into our lives. A simple pencil sharpener can become a symbol for pleasant childhood memories, memories of enjoying learning how to read and write our first alphabets. A lost coin newly found can be a symbol for wealth to come. The name badge from an old job can become a symbol of potential new employment.

Ancestral references quite naturally become our own as we interact with those of our immediate culture, deeply adopting the spiritual references of that culture. For instance, if one is born into a family with North European heritage, it is inevitable that he will see a sailing ship as a symbol of great adventure, an equal-sided hammer as a symbol of godly power, and a crow as a symbol of both death and pronouncement. These spiritually symbolic references are woven into the upbringing, guidance, and discipline that North European families mete out to their offspring.

Too, as we rub shoulders with new cultures, we adopt their symbols into our own spiritual caches as we learn about and embrace their histories. One who learns about the Inuit culture cannot resist sympathizing with the raw nature of the experiences and trials involved with the quest for sheer survival in a northernmost environment. As we learn about and develop love for the people of other cultures, we embrace their spirits with our own, and we eagerly take up their standards by, to some extent either slightly or extremely, emulating their lifestyles and holding their gods in regard.

By learning about other cultures and embracing the universal beauty in their experiences and symbols, we enrich our own spiritual lives and develop wisdom and ability to help a wider variety of people. As a healer, one who throws the bones will not be one who holds disdain for other cultures or paths. A sangoma who is a true healer and spiritual guide will operate out of love and truth, embracing other cultures and dispensing spiritual guidance in ways that all can understand.

By being a student of religion, spirituality, cultures, and healing, you will enhance your qualification to be a true sangoma. By practicing throwing the bones in a reverent manner, you will create opportunities to develop your sense of spiritual perception, become more and more familiar with your bones, and ingrain within yourself your own unique pattern of communicating priceless spiritual counsel. Practice each day, and very soon, you will gain the confidence, ability, and qualification needed to throw the bones for others.

When the time finally arrives for you to read for someone other than yourself, remember to see the querent as one that you deeply love. Remember to honor the Spirit that "drives" all spiritual counseling in the first place. Most of all, remember to give your best.

7 ETHICS

There are some who say that throwing the bones should be done only by those who are born into a direct lineage of ancestral sangomas. If this stark purist attitude were to be enforced across the entire board of spiritual practices, then no one would be allowed to walk the spiritual path of his choice. Most people on this planet are now born in cities without the luxury of a close "village" community and spiritual system. Are those people supposed to live spiritually austere lives? Are they not to partake of the avenue of prayer? Are only trained priests allowed to read the Bible and disseminate its teachings?

We live in an intricately connected world. More than ever before, we are able to partake of the knowledge and wisdom of a plethora of cultures. Unlike the ancient traveler who was forced to visit on foot, we have vast electronic means and jet-speed traveling options that can place us within the heart of a different culture within just a few moments.

Consider the progression of travel methods: first, we traveled by foot, then by horse, then by cart, by car, by plane, and now, by internet and video chats. The methods by which we embrace and assimilate other cultures, making some of them our very own, have progressed beautifully, and we must consider this a natural process of man's evolution. If you do not believe this, then why are you reading this book? If you are a professed spiritual traveler and believe that a contemporary sangoma cannot be born in a big city and live in a suburb, then it would be good to seriously inspect your beliefs. Every single thing that we do today is a contemporary act no matter where it originated, and the spreading out of quaint customs is a natural part of the evolution and success of the quaint, ancient communities that created those customs.

No matter your country or circumstance of origin, if you hear the call of Spirit to take up throwing the bones, preaching, painting, writing, or crunching numbers, you have the Spirit-given right to follow your calling. Do not allow yourself to feel daunted or guilty for doing what Spirit lovingly tells you to do. It is not only your right, but it is your responsibility to live your authentic life. Only by doing this will you achieve ultimate spiritual satisfaction!

If you do indeed decide to take up throwing the bones, it is important to consider your reputation from this point on. Throwing the bones, for now, is a very unique occupation, and not everyone embraces it or the people who practice it. Once you begin this very serious practice, it will be imperative that you remain true to the Spirit that offered the calling, and it will be imperative to emulate the fruitages that develop from walking in line with that Spirit.

Do you want to be considered as the "crazy person who throws the bones," or do you want to be considered a wise, loving person who is always ready to assist someone? If you have unsettled business with someone or a pressing need to pursue psychological therapy, then it is imperative to finish that business before taking on the challenges of becoming a sangoma. The words of an ancient Mystic, "Physician, heal thyself" come to mind; if you are not well yourself, then how can you reasonably expect to heal others?

If you desire fame and fortune to come to you from throwing the bones, then you need to put this book down and consider another occupation. Fame is highly overrated and is only for those who seek power over others; a sangoma's fame should only arise from having assisted many people in profound ways. If one is to be famous for anything, it should be for one's capacity for love and altruism. If one thinks that millions can be made by throwing the bones, then it would be good to know that I have yet to meet a sangoma who drives a Porsche, a BMW, or even a high end Ford. The only spiritually pure reason for a reader to become a sangoma is that one has been led by Spirit to provide loving spiritual guidance to people who honestly seek it.

Sometimes, sangomas can meet people who actually have addictions to readings. These unfortunate people seek spiritual counsel from multiple readers, many times asking the same questions over and over. When we meet people like this, it is important not to indulge their addiction, but to actually offer valuable spiritual guidance.

When we encounter someone with such a problem, we must absolutely focus on core spiritual subjects. If the querent's question is about when a lover will text, we will do well to find a way to address why they feel the need for quick response and what they can develop within themselves to weather through periods of "unknowing." If the question is about when they will make a million dollars, then we will do well to address why they are not happy with what they already have. If they ask if a perceived enemy will ever reap his karma or just desserts, we will do well to address why the querent is so keen to see punishment enacted on someone and why forgiveness and a "letting go" have not yet occurred.

Spiritual guidance does not usually come in the form of "yes, Sergio is your soul mate" or "yes, you will make a million dollars." It comes in the form of "your key to happiness is confidence in your own self" and "developing a sense of gratitude and realizing what you actually need is the key to acknowledging the richness of your life."

Finally, charging for services is an important part of throwing the bones. In this Universe, there must be an equal exchange of energy in order for an interaction to be sanctioned by Spirit, and yet many people seem to expect spiritual readers, musicians, artists, and baby sitters to work without adequate payment. Some people would pay a thousand dollars for a famous architect to design a doghouse and yet illegally rip a musician's work from the internet without shame. One would not expect a carpenter to come over and nail even a few boards for free. One would not expect an engineer or architect to design even a doghouse without being paid for services rendered. Likewise, one must not expect someone who works in a spiritual practice to work for free. Work is life, life is energy, and, today, money represents a certain amount of life energy that has been used to generate the money.

If you have questions about how much to charge, it would be good to remember that most readers charge about one dollar a minute for any type of reading. If a querent were to call a national call line or psychic line, he would expect to pay from three to ten dollars per minute! When we realize this fact, we can see that the charge of one dollar per minute is more than reasonable, and in fact, it is a "steal."

Always have the question of payment taken care of before the reading begins. This is a huge test for those who suffer from low self-esteem and are hesitant to ask for money from anyone for services rendered. The underlying reason for this is that they themselves do not value their work! Therefore, remember to see the value in what you do, and realize, too, that unless you state up front what you expect to be paid, then your communication will be less than honest.

Consider this: a reader spends one exhaustive hour at a friend's house, giving him a reading and afterward, discussing options and solutions for life's difficulties. If the reader is new, then this is inevitably going to happen if he has not learned to set good boundaries on his time and energy. However, once a reader has provided a number of readings and is experienced enough to be able to understand the energy that readings require, and yet still does not voice a fixed price and time limit before a reading, then that reader will not progress. The reason is that the reader has a masochistic desire to sacrifice himself for something that has absolutely no guarantee of fulfillment. How can I say that? It is because the querent will always heed the reader's counsel in direct proportion to the amount that he has paid for it. If he has paid nothing, then he will not respect or value it.

Put a price on your time and energy, and then give people more than their money's worth.

8 PERSONAL NOTES

Every single day, I awaken with an alchemical task: to weigh the spiritual climate of the awakening world and assimilate my emotions about doing what I do. You see, there's not one single day that passes in which I do not wake up with both the elevating joy from people whom I have helped and the looming weight of the fundamentalist world's judgment of the gift that has been bestowed upon me, freely and without my asking for it. The Light and love that abides in my heart fuels my spiritual journey, while the weight of the world is on my heart. I love everyone in this world. The ones that I help are wonderfully vocal in their appreciation, while the ones who are afraid are so loud in their negative judgment.

When a preacher asks all to pray with him, who does he think that the prayer is supposed to reach? The Spirit. When that preacher recounts experiences of people who have seen the Light, who does he think is responsible for that Light? Spirit.

When a twin claims that he can sense what his sibling is feeling, even from long distances away, that is accepted by society, even by religious groups.

When a mother claims that she can tell what her child is feeling, even from distances away, people know that it is true. When a friend just "knows" that she needs to call another friend, everyone accepts that spiritual connection. It is my prayer that one day more people will appreciate the spiritual gifts that God has bestowed on everyone, each with his own particular gift.

Each one is born to a particular quadrant on this planet, and each one of us is born into a society which allows exposure to its particular spiritual atmosphere. As a practitioner of a Western Mystic Tradition, I call upon Jesus and the Archangels each day. If I were to have been born in another hemisphere, I would be calling upon Spirit in a different way.

Over the years, a wide variety of querents have come to me for answers. Each one has taught me something, and I have honestly given them my best. Each one has a need unique to his own situation. Each one is a loved, precious spirit in this beautiful universe.

It is also my prayer that each of you dear readers grow and blossom beautifully in your lives. Remember that you have the right to live your genuine authentic lives, and all you have to do is to gather up the courage and adrenaline, and then just do it! If I can help you in any way, do not hesitate to reach out to me. Every blessing to you and yours!

ABOUT THE AUTHOR

Cindy Rhodes
RM3 SC HHP ATLC AADP

is a mystic, musician, artist, traveler, student, teacher and helper of many. As a mystic in a Western Mystery Tradition and a devotee of Inuit spiritualism, she embraces both the Hebrew-based Tree of Life as a symbol for her life path and the goddess Sedna as a symbol for all women, reminding us that suffering can breed creativity and that without challenges, we are but mindless dust. As a Reiki Master, Spiritual Counselor, Holistic Healthcare Practitioner, Art Therapy Life Coach, and member of the American Association of Drugless Practitioners, she uses her time, talents, and possessions to assist all that she can and works to bring love, joy, and peace to people in entertaining ways. Remembering that this particular life is not for forever, she reminds us to live life to the fullest and to never ever stop learning.